MILITARY UNIFORMS & WEAPONRY
-THE POSTER BOOK OF-
World War I

This 1987 edition
published by Military Press
distributed by Crown Publishers, Inc.,
225 Park Avenue South,
New York, New York 10003

Created by David Graves
Designed by Crispin Goodall

ISBN 0-517-64473-8

Printed in Italy

MILITARY UNIFORMS & WEAPONRY
–THE POSTER BOOK OF–
World War I

90 Authentic Figures in Color   Illustrated by Pierre Turner
INTRODUCTION BY ANDREW MOLLO

MILITARY PRESS
NEW YORK

Although today World War I is often remembered for its senseless massacre of young soldiers, sent to die in their thousands by silly-looking old generals with walrus moustaches, it was in fact more interesting and significant than that. It radically altered the whole concept of warfare in which not only the army, but the whole nation – its science, technology and morale – was put to the supreme test. Nor did the war really end with the last shot, because in its wake it brought political and social upheaval on such an unprecedented scale, that in many ways we are still feeling its repercussions to this day.

From the military point of view it was the small feuding Balkan countries which entered the war with the most experience and the least illusions. The great European powers, elated by colourful parades and spectacular summer manouevres, went to war with a display of enthusiasm which has never been repeated since. They were confident that their splendidly uniformed and magnificently drilled men would bring the war to a speedy conclusion in time for Christmas. But then, with the exception of an odd colonial skirmish against primitively armed natives, Europe's armies had little or no recent experience of actual warfare.

These bush wars however brought about one basic and fundamental awareness which was, that brightly coloured and tight-fitting uniforms were not best suited to modern warfare. Many British officers were advised to visit their outfitters before leaving for the colonies. There they could equip themselves with sturdy and comfortable clothing in muted colours, which had been designed for stalking and shooting game.

Once in the colonies the more enterprising officers – freed from the restraints and hidebound conservatism of their less adventurous fellows – 'went native'. They adopted the style of clothing, equipment, and even arms of their adversaries, and so khaki (a Persian word meaning earth) uniforms were developed, first in the colonies, and later for wear in Europe. By the outbreak of war most countries – with three notable exceptions – had protective coloured uniforms, be it the tobacco brown of Bulgaria or the German field-grey.

The notable exceptions were Austro-Hungary, France, and Belgium. Unlike France and Belgium who should really have known better, Austria was not a colonial empire in the global sense. In 1909 Austria introduced a pike-grey uniform which was so simple and practical, and so modern in its silhouette, that even today its influence can still be recognised. However parsimony and conservatism continued to assert their influence. In 1864 Austrian Emperor Franz Joseph's brother Maximilian was made Emperor of Mexico. He immediately reorganised the army, and ordered an enormous quantity of madder uniform cloth from his homeland.

Before it could be shipped he was deposed and the cloth was no longer required. After a number of suggestions, it was decided to use up the material by giving the Austrian cavalry madder trousers. It is not recorded how the idea was originally received, but when it was proposed that they should be replaced by grey trousers, the Emperor was petitioned, and as a special privilege, the cavalry were allowed to retain their red trousers until 1915.

France, despite her colonial experience, and numerous attempts to modernise her uniforms, went to war in 1914 in blue and red. Contrary to popular belief red trousers were neither traditionally French, nor the brainchild of a sartorially motivated monarch. The decision to introduce them was purely commercial. France had invented a fast red dye and wanted to break England's monopoly in this commodity. What better way to advertise this new expertise than to dress the army in red trousers.

Also for the first time a country's industrial capacity was to play a decisive role in the war. The ability to manufacture, not only guns, but all the other paraphernalia of war from uniforms to bandages, meant that only the highly developed industrial nations could sustain a war for any length of time. Countries like France, Germany, and Great Britain had to supply not only their own needs, but those of their allies as well. France probably took on a greater burden than any other country, and stamped out the Adrian steel helmet by the million. She completely re-equipped the Serbian Army well into the mid-1920's. Britain's ability to weave seemingly endless bales of cloth, enabled the Portuguese to replace their grey uniforms with ones made in England, and the Belgians – although not all that keen on khaki – adopted it as a colour for their new uniforms in 1915 simply because Britain alone could supply the enormous quantity of cloth required.

Enormous increases in the rapidity and accuracy of fire during the second half of the nineteenth century not only brought about the bloody stalemate that epitomised World War I, but exercised a terrific influence on two very important aspects of a soldier's appearance. Rapidity of fire meant that he carried much more ammunition, and so the old shoulder-belt equipment was replaced by one based on the waistbelt, from which one, two, or even three ammunition pouches could be suspended, as well as the other bits and pieces that a soldier had to carry.

Accuracy of both small arms and artillery, and the nature of the war in which mostly the head was exposed, caused a disproportionate number of head injuries. The French heavy cavalryman with his metal helmet was to be envied, while his less fortunate brothers in the infantry found the little round steel skull cap which they were supposed to wear under the kepi, useful for every purpose other than the one for which it was intended. A French *Intendance* Department officer, August-Louis Adrian designed and had produced a steel helmet which was the first of the many that were to follow.

In April 1915 during the Battle of Ypres, the Germans successfully used poisonous chlorine gas for the first time, and so began chemical warfare. Although a failure as an offensive weapon, it obliged the Allies to divert vast amounts of time and money into developing and supplying gas masks and other decontamination equipment, which could have been more usefully employed elsewhere. The first gas mask was no more than a nose-clip and cotton wool mouth pad which had been soaked in sodium carbonate, sodium thiosulphate and water, but by the end of the war, when Britan alone had manufactured, 50,000,000 gas masks, they had become quite a sophisticated apparatus.

Paradoxically although the American Civil War may lay some claim to the title, the first of the fully scientific wars was also to see the revival of medieval methods of warfare. After the initial weeks of movement, both sides dug in a short distance apart, and for the next four years waged a bitter trench warfare in which they threw, catapulted, and fired a whole range of missiles at each other. Then dressed in various kinds of protective clothing and even body armour, they assaulted and killed each other even with clubs, maces and daggers.

Flying also came into its own during World War I, and even the cynics who at first viewed aviators in much the same way as motorists – as show-offs – came to realise that yet another decisive weapon was in the making.

Since the best mechanics were to be found in the engineers, it was logical that military aviation began as a branch of that service. In 1910 the French formed their air ship and aviation services into an autonomous corps, and the British followed in 1912. But nowhere during World War I was there to be found a completely independent air arm, until Britain amalgamated her naval and flying corps into the Royal Air Force in April 1918.

Most armies employed semi-official volunteer corps who were mainly involved in motor transport (Italy and Austro-Hungary) and the medical services (Red Cross, etc). For the most part these organisation were uniformed and used their own system of rank badges, while the Royal and Imperial Austro-Hungarian Volunteer Automobile Corps, wore army rank badges on the collar, and corps rank badges on the cuffs. Unfortunately space will not permit the many and varied uniforms of these and many other organisations to be covered in this book.

1 Austria: Pioneer, Infantry Regiment 49, summer field dress, 1915
The uniform is the standard one for non-mounted personnel, with the special trousers which ended in a cloth anklet which fastened with buttons.

Equipment: As a pioneer he carries – in addition to his infantry equipment – a long-handled shovel and axe.

Weapons: Austrian 8 mm. Mannlicher M.1895 repeating rifle.

2 Austria: Cadet Sergeant (Feldwebel) Infantry Regiment 84, summer 1915
As a one-year volunteer he was entitled to wear the gold lace on the cuff, and as an *Aspirant* sergeant, the officers' sword with yellow silk knot.

Equipment: Standard pattern other ranks' belt with brass buckle.

Weapons: Automatic pistol and sword.

3 Austria: Rifleman, Landesschützen Regiment 1, field dress, 1915
In recognition of their bravery in action these units were collectively re-named *Kaiserschützen* in 1917. The uniform was standard, except that pantaloons for wear with woollen stockings replaced long trousers. On the left side of the cap all ranks wore a cock feather plume, and on the breast the marksmens' lanyard for those entitled to it.

Equipment: Standard infantry equipment with rucksack instead of pack, and special mountaineering equipment.

Weapons: Austrian 8 mm. Carbine (*Stützen*) M.95.

1 *Pioneer* 2 *Officer cadet* 3 *Rifleman*

4 *Dragoon*   5 *Lancer officer*   6 *Lancer officer*

4 Austria: Dragoon, Dragoon Regiment No. 5, exercise order, 1914

Soon after the beginning of the war the distinctive head-dress was withdrawn, and the red side cap, which was standard for all cavalry regiments, was worn instead.

Equipment: Standard waistbelt, ammunition pouches and waterbottle suspended from leather strap over right shoulder.

Weapons: Austrian 8 mm. Steyr-Mannlicher M.1890 carbine, and M.1869 cavalry sabre.

5 Austria: Major, Lancer (Ulan) Regiment No. 3 in 'Kommoder' or exercise order, 1914

He wears the undress *Kappi*, and *Pelz* with gold lace on the cuffs which distinguished him as a field officer.

Weapons: M.1861/69 cavalry officers' sabre.

6 Austria: 2nd Lieutenant, Lancer Regiment No. 6, field service order, August 1914

This officer wears the *Waffenrock* with shirt collar turned up and over the tunic collar.

Equipment: Standard waistbelt, binoculars in case, and water-bottle suspended from sword belt which was worn under the tunic.

Weapons: Austrian 8 mm. Roth-Steyr automatic pistol in brown leather holster which was suspended from a strap over the left shoulder, and M.1861/69 cavalry officers' sabre.

7 Austria: Officer Cadet (Fähnrich), Dragoon Regiment No. 3, exercise order, 1916
Over his tunic he wears the field-grey version of the *Pelz*. The legs and seat of the breeches for mounted personnel were lined with leather.

Equipment: Standard waistbelt and pistol holster.

Weapons: Automatic pistol, and M.1861/69 cavalry sabre.

8 Austria: 2nd Lieutenant (Leutnant) of cavalry, Siebenburgen, 1916
Off-duty this officer wears the side cap, blouse, and *antrasit* grey breeches. The shoulder cord or *Schlinge* was worn by officers only on the left shoulder.

9 Austria: Squadron Pionier, Dragoon Regiment No. 3, field service dress, 1915
The summer version of the field blouse was made of grey cotton drill. Normally mounted personnel wore brown leather gaiters.

Equipment: Standard waistbelt.

Weapons: Austrian 8 mm. Ster-Mannlicher M.1890 carbine, and M.1853 Pioneer sword-bayonet.

7 *Officer cadet*   8 *Cavalry officer*   9 *Cavalry pionier*

10 *Infantryman*   11 *Hussar n.c.o.*   12 *Gendarmerie n.c.o.*

10 Hungary: Private, Royal Hungarian Infantry Regiment No. 1 in 'Kommoder' dress, 1914

This is the standard M.1909 pike-grey field service dress with the special trousers for Hungarian dismounted personnel.

Equipment: Standard waistbelt with brass buckle bearing Hungarian coat of arms.

Weapons: Austrian Mannlicher M.1895 bayonet.

11 Hungary: Sergeant (Wachtmeister), Royal Hungarian Hussar Regiment No. 4, field service order, 1914

The Attila, Pelz and breeches of Hungarian Hussars were trimmed with red, and Austrian Hussars yellow braid.

Equipment: Standard waistbelt and automatic pistol holster suspended from strap over the left shoulder.

Weapons: Austrian 8 mm. Roth-Steyr automatic pistol, and M.1869 cavalry sabre.

12 Hungary: Sergeant (Wachtmeister II klasse), Royal Hungarian Gendarmerie service dress, 1914

The distinctive feature of this uniform was the black brimmed hat adorned with cock feathers. The chevrons on the left forearm denote a long serving volunteer n.c.o.

Equipment: Standard pattern waistbelt and ammunition pouches.

Weapons: Russia 7·62 mm. Moisin-Nagrant rifle (carbine) and bayonet, and M.1861 infantry pattern short-sword with n.c.o.s' knot.

13 Bulgaria: Private of Infantry, Uskub, Macedonia, 1914

This infantryman wears the typical tobacco-brown field uniform with cap band and piping, and shoulder straps in the infantry arm-of-service colour.

Equipment: Standard waistbelt and ammunition pouch.

Weapons: Mannlicher 8 mm. repeating rifle M.1895.

14 Bulgaria: General Jekoff, Macedonia, 1917

As Commander-in-Chief on the Bulgarian Army, Jekoff wears the peace-time greatcoat, which was almost identical to the Russian pattern.

Equipment: Officers' waistbelt.

Weapons: Bayonet with brown leather knot.

15 Bulgaria: Colonel of Infantry, 10th Bulgarian Division, Drama, May 1917

The similarity between this and the Russian uniform, from which it was derived, is very noticeable. He wears the Order of Bravery 4th Class.

Equipment: Officers' waistbelt, pistol lanyard and binoculars in their case.

13 *Infantryman*   14 *General*   15 *Infantry officer*

16 *Mountain rifleman*   17 *General*   18 *Infantryman*

16 France: Private 1st Class, 14th Battalion Mountain Rifles, 1914
Over his dark-blue beret he wears a white cover. The French horn on the sleeve distinguished him as a marksman.

Equipment: Standard French infantry equipment and Alpine stick.

17 France: General Foch, Commander-in-Chief of the Armies of The Somme, 1915
Foch wears the service dress tunic which was introduced in 1906, with the order of the *Légion d'Honneur*. Rank distinctions appear on the kepi, and on the cuffs.

18 France: Private, 54th Regiment of Infantry of the Line, France, September 1914
This typical *biffin* wears the kepi with cover under which he wore from 1915 a steel skull cap or *cervellière* of which some six million were produced. It was not unknown for the bright-red trousers to be concealed beneath blue overalls as well.

Equipment: Standard infantry other ranks' waistbelt with M.1877 ammunition pouches and haversack. The M.1893 pack with shelter half and invidiual mess–tin strapped to its top.

Weapons: French 8 mm. 'Lebel' Rifle M.1886/93 and bayonet.

19 France: Lieutenant on the General Staff of General Passaga, near Hardaumont, 1915
This staff officer wears one of the many different patterns of horizon-blue tunic with special general staff collar patches, and the Military Medal on the left breast.

20 Marshal Foch, France, 23 August 1918
On the day that Foch was promoted to the rank of Marshal of France, he wore horizon-blue service dress with the peace-time kepi.

Equipment: Waistbelt and cross strap for officers.

Weapons: M.1845 (Modified 1855) sabre for senior officers.

21 France: Private 1st Class, 115th Regiment of Infantry, France, 1917
This rifleman (*Voltigeur*) wears the standard M.1915 field uniform with greatcoat, and Adrian steel helmet. The chevrons on the left sleeve indicated private 1st class – each stripe representing six months' service.

Equipment: Standard infantry equipment and Tissot gas mask in its metal container.

Weapons: French 8 mm. 'Lebel' M.1886/93 rifle and bayonet.

19 *Staff officer*　　　　　　　　20 *Marshal of France*　　　　　　　　21 *Infantryman*

22 *Infantryman*   23 *Colonel of rifles*   24 *Engineer corporal*

22 France: Private of Infantry near Houthem, 10 September, 1917
Uniform as for previous figure.

Equipment: Full marching order here consists of pack with mess-tin, rolled blanket and shelter-half, spare boots, three haversacks, gas mask, water-bottle and an axe.

Weapons: French 8 mm. 'Lebel' M.1886/93 rifle and bayonet.

23 France: Colonel Driant, Commander 56th and 59th Rifle Battalions, Verdun, 1916
This famous officer, who defended the wood at Caures for 24 hours, wears the M.1886 officers' tunic with rifles pantaloons. On the breast he wears both the Legion of Honour and the Croix de Guerre.

Equipment: Waistbelt and pistol holster on the right hip.

Weapons: French 8 mm. revolver M.1892 for officers.

24 France: Corporal of Engineers, Vincennes, July 1917
Engineers were distinguished by the special badge on the steel helmet, and the colour of the collar patches. From the 1st to the 15th of the month the greatcoat was worn buttoned on the right, and from the 16th to the 31st on the left. This was done to ensure equal wear on the garment.

Equipment: Standard infantry equipment, and shovel with long handle.

Weapons: French 8 mm. 'Lebel' M.1886/93 rifle and bayonet.

25 France: 2nd Lieutenant, Assault Artillery, France, 1918
This tank commander wears the Adrian helmet with artillery badge, and leather coat for motor vehicle drivers. In August 1918 a special sleeve badge consisting of crossed cannons surmounted by a knight's helmet was introduced for crews of tanks.

Equipment: Standard M.1915 waistbelt and automatic pistol holster.

Weapons: French 7·65 mm. Ruby automatic pistol.

26 France: Gunner, 13th Field Artillery Regiment, Vincennes, September 1916
Standard horizon-blue field uniform with tunic (*vareuse*), and greatcoat rolled and worn over the shoulder.

Equipment: Standard M.1915 brown leather equipment, haversack and gas mask in metal cannister.

Weapons: French 8 mm. M.1890 (second type) carbine.

27 France: Driver, horse-drawn vehicle, Vincennes, 1916
He wears the obsolete greatcoat under a fur waistcoat, sheepskin mittens, waterproof overalls and wooden clogs.

25 *Tank officer*   26 *Artilleryman*   27 *Waggon driver*

28 *Trumpet-Major*   29 *The Kaiser*   30 *Field-Marshal*

28 Prussia: Staff Trumpet-Major (Sergeant), 1st Troop Life Gendarmerie, near Tarnopol, 24 July 1917

The troop of Gendarmes that acted as a Royal Escort retained their peace-time uniforms, even after they had become officially obsolete.

Equipment: Special pattern belt and buckle and bandolier with cartridge box.

Weapons: German 9 mm. Parabellum (Lüger) 08 automatic pistol in holster, and M.1889 cavalry sword.

29 Prussia: His Royal and Imperial Majesty Emperor (Kaiser) William the Second, near Tarnopol, 24 July 1917

As Chief of the Army he wears the uniform of the 1st Foot Guards of which he was Colonel-in-Chief (*Chef*).

Equipment: Standard Prussian officers' waistbelt and unusual straps supporting.

Weapons: Pistol in holster, and M.1889 officers' sword.

30 Prussia: His Excellency General Field Marshal von Beneckendorff und von Hindenburg, near Noyon, June 1918

As Chief-of-Staff Hindenburg wears the regimental uniform of the 3rd Foot Guards but with the badges of rank of a *General-Feldmarschall*. In his left hand he carries the service version of the baton (*Interimstab*).

31 Prussia: Landwehr infantryman near Brussels, 1914

The pace-time greatcoat is here being worn with collar patches, but no shoulder straps. The spiked helmet was made less conspicuous and protected from the weather by a cloth cover.

Equipment: Standard waistbelt with M.1895 pouches.

Weapons: German 7·9 mm. rifle 88 with M.1871 bayonet.

32 Prussia: Lieutenant, Flügeladjutant to the Kaiser, near Riga, September 1917

As an A.D.C. he wears Guard *Litzen* on the collar and cuffs, the royal cypher on the shoulder straps, aiguilette and *Lampassen* on the breeches.

Equipment: Standard officers' waistbelt and pistol holster.

Weapons: Automatic pistol.

33 Prussia: Private, 4th Foot Guard Regiment, Berlin, August 1914

This is the standard M.1910 field uniform with guard *Litzen* on the collar and cuffs.

Equipment: Standard waistbelt with M.1909 ammunition pouches and entrenching tool, and M.1895 pack.

Weapons: M.84/98 bayonet.

31 *Infantryman*   32 *A.D.C.*   33 *Guardsman*

34 *Artilleryman*   35 *Field Marshal*   36 *Infantryman*

34 Bavaria: Mounted driver, Bavarian Field Artillery, 1915
The uniform is standard M.1910 except that Bavarian artillery wore the spike instead of the ball on the helmet.

Equipment: Standard waistbelt for mounted personnel and revolver holster.

Weapons: German 10.55 mm. Reichsrevolver M.1883 and Bavarian pattern artillery sabre.

35 Bavaria: His Royal Highness Prince Rupprecht of Bavaria, Western Front, June, 1918
As Commander of the 6th Army, Prince Rupprecht wears the uniform of a Bavarian Field Marshal with special pattern collar patches for Bavarian general officers.

Equipment: Standard pattern Bavarian officers' waistbelt.

Weapons: Bavarian officers' sword.

36 Bavaria: Private, Bavarian Infantry Life Regiment, 1916
He wears the simplified M.1910 tunic with plain cuffs. When the standardized M.1915 uniform was introduced, Bavarians were distinguished from personnel in other contingents, by a white and light-blue lace on the collar.

Equipment: Standard infantry equipment with M.1909 ammunition pouches, flashlight and 'Alpen' stick.

Weapons: German 7·9 mm. rifle 98 with M.84/98 bayonet.

37 Prussia: Corporal (Unteroffizier) Landsturm Battalion 68, Berlin, 1914

The shako is the M.1860. The roman numeral on the collar indicated the army corps to which the unit (indicated by arabic numerals) belonged.

Equipment: Standard other ranks' waistbelt with M.1889 ammunition pouches, and M.1887 pack and straps.

Weapons: German 7·9 mm. Mauser Gewehr 88 and 71/84 bayonet.

38 German Reich: Major, 3rd Landsturm Squadron VII Army Corps (Uhlan Regiment No. 5), Belgium, 1926

This is the standard M.1910 uniform for lancer officers, while the *Czapka* plate bears the Landsturm cross in the centre.

Equipment: Non-regulation pattern belt.

39 German Reich: Private, Landsturm Infantry Battalion, No. 49, Poland, 1915

All men between the ages of 17 and 45 who were found unfit for war service were incorporated into the Landsturm units, who if passed as fit for garrison duty were armed. Their distinctive head-dress was the black oilskin cap with the Landsturm cross on the front.

Equipment: Standard waistbelt with M.1889 ammunition pouches.

Weapons: German 7·9 mm. Mauser Gewehr 98 and bayonet.

37 *Landwehr n.c.o.*   38 *Landsturm lancer officer*   39 *Landsturm man*

40 *Brigadier General*   41 *Field Marshal*   42 *Brigadier General*

40 Great Britain: Brigadier General F. W. Ramsey, commanding the Irish Brigade, 16th Division, France, June 1917
Many private firms produced steel helmets, and this example was supplied covered with cloth, and with a general officers' cap badge on the front. The red armlet indicated divisional headquarters.

Equipment: Sam Browne belt with small haversack.

41 Great Britain: Field Marshal Sir Douglas Haig, K.T., G.C.B., G.C.V.O., K.C.I.E., British Headquarters, Château Beauquesne, France, 1916
Haig wears a khaki field service cap with field marshal's cap badge.

Equipment: Sam Browne belt, and camera in case suspended from a strap over the left shoulder.

42 Great Britain: Brigadier General, Nesle, Battle of Bapaume, 25 March 1918
On an other ranks' cap he wears his shoulder strap rank badge which was quite unauthorised. The oak-leaf embroidery on the gorget patches was worn by all general officers unless they were on the staff of H.Q. General Staff, in which case they wore gold chain gimp.

Equipment: Sam Browne belt.

43 Great Britain: Company Sergeant Major, King's Company, 1st Battalion Grenadier Guards, London, 1915
This is the 1902 pattern khaki or service drab uniform on the British Army with the stiff peaked cap.

Equipment: 1908 pattern web equipment and binoculars in brown leather case suspended from strap over right shoulder.

Weapons: British ·303 S.M.L.E. Mark I rifle.

44 Great Britain: Lieutenant Colonel A. E. Cator, Brigade Staff Officer, 20th Brigade, France, 21 November 1914
Cator wears the cap (with khaki cover) and gorget patches of a substantive colonel, and the special tunic of his regiment, the Scots Guards.

Equipment: Sam Browne belt and sword frog.

45 Great Britain: 2nd Lieutenant, King's Company, 1st Battalion Grenadier Guards, London, 1915
In the Brigade of Guards, and Household Cavalry, officers wore their badges on the shoulder straps throughout the war.

Equipment: Sam Browne belt; water-bottle suspended from brown leather strap over the left shoulder, and haversack over both shoulders.

Weapons: British Enfield ·380; pistol No. 2 Mark I in holster, and Foot Guards officers' pattern 1854 sword, with the M.1895 blade.

43 *Foot Guards n.c.o.*   44 *Foot Guards officer*   45 *Foot Guards subaltern*

46 Infantryman   47 Infantry officer   48 Infantryman

46 Great Britain: Private of Infantry, Bernafay Wood, November 1916
The leather jerkin was one of the many types of winter clothing issued to troops in the trenches.

Equipment: 1914-pattern leather equipment and empty sandbag for carrying grenades.

Weapons: British ·303 S.M.L.E. Mark I rifle with canvas breech cover.

47 Great Britain: 2nd Lieutenant Oliver, 2nd Battalion Durham Light Infantry, 'Hobb's Farm', Houplines, spring 1915
The field service cap was unusual, but as a sniper Oliver probably found it more practical than the peaked cap.

Weapons: ·303 Ross sporting rifle.

48 Great Britain: Private, The King's Own (Royal Lancaster Regiment), St Eloi, 27 March 1916
The soft version of the peaked cap with earflaps was christened 'Gor blimey' (God blind me) by the troops. The crossed flags denoted a trained signaller.

Equipment: 1914-pattern web equipment with October 1914 modification to the lower left ammunition pouches, and P helmet gas mask in its canvas bag which was introduced in December 1915.

Weapons: British ·303 S.M.L.E. Mark I rifle.

49 Great Britain: Sergeant Hay, 2nd Battalion Argyll and Sutherland Highlanders, Bois Grenier section of the front, March 1915

Hay wears the standard single-breasted 'coats, great, dismounted men', and the Glengarry cap.

Equipment: 1908-pattern web equipment.

Weapons: British ·303 S.M.L.E. Mark I rifle.

50 Great Britain: Major, 2nd Battalion Highland Light, Infantry, Cologne, April 1919

The head-dress is the tam-o'-shanter which replaced the Balmoral bonnet with khaki cover in September 1915, for all Highland regiments. Highlanders usually rounded the corners of the front of their tunics, while officers wore the doublet with the rank distinctions on the so-called gauntlet cuff.

Equipment: Sam Browne belt with binoculars in case.

Weapons: British ·455 Webley Mark 6 pistol in holster.

51 Great Britain: Private, 10th Battalion Argyll and Sutherland Highlanders, Cologne, April 1919

The cap badge on the tam-o'-shanter was usually placed on a square of material in the regimental tartan. The circular badge denoted the brigade (97th), the colour of bars the company (B), and the number of bars the seniority of the regiment within the brigade.

Equipment: 1908-pattern web equipment with small box respirator in its bag on to of the large pack. The piece of wood next to the bayonet scabbard is an entrenching tool haft.

Weapons: British ·303 S.M.L.E. Mark I rifle.

49 *Highland n.c.o.*   50 *Highland officer*   51 *Highlander*

52 *Ration carrier*   53 *Private soldier*   54 *Medical orderly*

52 Great Britain: Private soldier carrying food container, Arras, March 1917
Over his khaki tunic he wears one of the many types of fur coat and jerkins which were issued as additional – and very necessary – winter clothing.

Equipment: Food container, and 1914-pattern leather equipment, and small box respirator.

53 Great Britain: Private soldier, Tunnelling Company Royal Engineers, St Pierre Divion, November 1916
Ponchos and thigh gum boots were issued as and when required from unit or formation stores, and were not general issue.

Equipment: P.H. (Phenate-Hexane) helmet-type gas mask in carrying bag.

54 Great Britain: Private, Royal Army medical Corps, Cologne, 24 April 1919
1st and 2nd Class orderlies had one or two bars respectively of cherry-coloured braid.

Equipment: 1908-pattern web equipment without ammunition pouches, but with additional satchels for medical equipment, etc.

55 Great Britain: Air Mechanic, Royal Flying Corps, full marching order 1918
This is the original uniform introduced in 1911, with the 'Austrian' pattern field service cap, and 'maternity' jacket with badge for qualified observers which was introduced in November 1915 by AMO 404.

Equipment: 1908-pattern web equipment with leather ammunition pouch and revolver holster.

Weapons: British ·455 Webley Mark 6 pistol.

56 Great Britain: Captain W. G. Barker, No. 66 Squadron, Italy, 1918
Barker wears army service dress with the cap badge and collar 'dogs' of the Canadian Manitoba Regiment, into which he was originally commissioned. The R.F.C. wings were introduced in February 1913 by AO 40. The ribbon is that of the Military Cross.

Equipment: Officers' Sam Browne belt.

57 Great Britain: Captain, 2nd Brigade Royal Air Force, Château Nieppe, France, 6 August 1918
After the formation of the R.A.F., khaki service dress continued to be worn for the duration of the war although those officers possessing the new light-blue uniform could wear it as a mess dress. New rank badges were introduced in April 1918, but it was not until August 1919 that R.A.F. titles were finally adopted.

55 Observer   56 Pilot officer   57 Observer officer

58 *Infantry officer*   59 *Major General*   60 *Infantryman*

58 Greece: Lieutenant of Infantry, field service order, Salonika, September 1916
He wears the new-pattern peaked cap which gradually replaced the kepi worn in 59.

Equipment: Leather waistbelt and revolver holster, binoculars in case suspended from strap over the right, and water-bottle from strap over the left shoulder.

59 Greece: Major General, service dress, Athens, 1917
Notice the difference in cut between this tunic and the one illustrated in 58. The kepi is the old pattern, while the crowned cockade was standard for all ranks in the whole army.

Equipment: Sam Browne-type belt.

60 Greece: Private of Infantry, 6th division, field service order, Salonika, 18 September 1916
This is the typical field uniform of the Greek Army, but with cotton drill fatigue trousers, and puttees instead of the more usual gaiters.

Equipment: Standard infantry patterns.

Weapons: Austrian 6·5 mm. Mannlicher-Schönauer M.1903/14 and bayonet.

61 Poland: Lancer Mieczyslaw Selecki, 1 Squadron Polish Lancers, 1915
This full dress uniform which was worn for a short time, was privately purchased by the wearers. In action they wore Russian khaki field uniform with blue breeches with crimson *Lampassen*. On the crimson shoulder straps were the letter L and P interlaced. The cap lines were correctly worn on the left shoulder.

Weapons: Russian (French pattern) M.1826 cavalry sabre.

62 Poland: General of division Jósef Haller, France, 23 August 1918
As commander of the Polish Army in France, Haller wears a unique uniform combining French and Polish features.

Equipment: Sam Browne-type belt.

Weapons: French M.1845 (modified 1855) sabre for senior officers.

63 Poland: Private 1st Class, 3rd Polish Rifle Regiment, 1st Polish Rifle Division, France
The square-topped *Czapka* was worn without peak or chin strap by all non-mounted other ranks. All officers and mounted other ranks wore the same cap with peak and chin strap. The rest of the uniform was standard French.

Equipment: Standard French infantry equipment.

61 *Lancer*   62 *General of Division*   63 *Rifleman*

64 *Infantry n.c.o.*   65 *Staff officer*   66 *Artilleryman*

64 Portugal: Sergeant, 19th Infantry Regiment, Locon, France, 24 June 1917
The special steel helmet was made in Birmingham under contract from the Portuguese government. Replacement uniforms were also manufactured in England.

Equipment: Portuguese version of the British 1908-pattern web equipment which was introduced in 1911, and British small box respirator.

Weapons: British ·303 S.M.L.E. Mark I rifle with web breech cover, and bayonet.

65 Portugal: Captain, General Staff, Neuve-Chapelle, 25 June, 1917
This officer on tour of inspection with the British Liaison Staff wears very unofficial shirt-sleeve order with English shirt.

Equipment: British small box respirator.

66 Portugal: Gunner, Field Artillery, Roffey Camp, Sussex, England
Artillerymen were identified by the crossed cannons on their cap, while the type of artillery (field, heavy, fortress, etc.) by the badge on the collar.

Equipment: Standard artillery-pattern leather equipment.

67 Russia: Captan (Sotnik), His Imperial Majesty's Own Escort (Convoi), Mogilev, 8 March 1917

This is the war-time version of the black *Cherkesska* which was often made from greatcoat material. Note also the soft shoulder straps which were typical.

Weapons: Caucasian-pattern dagger (*Kindjal*) and sword (*Shashka*).

68 Russia: His Imperial Majesty Emperor Nicholas II of all Russias, as Colonel-in-Chief (Chef), Life Guard Imperial Family Rifle Regiment, Mogilev, 1916

On his cap he wears the special regimental-pattern cockade on which was superimposed the Reserve cross. He also wears shoulder-strap cyphers and aiguillette as former A.D.C. (*Flügeladjutant*) to his Father Alexander III.

Equipment: Standard pattern waistbelt.

69 Russia: Infantry officer, field service order, 1914

As the illustration shows, the back of both the tunic and shirt were quite plain, although the original tunic introduced in 1907 had piped back pocket flaps with four buttons.

Equipment: Standard officers' leather equipment with braces and sword slings.

Weapons: Russian 1909 pattern officers' sword which was worn suspended from the back of the scabbard in the Oriental manner.

67 *Cossack officer*   68 *The Tsar*   69 *Infantry officer*

70 *Guards officer*   71 *Major General*   72 *Guards n.c.o.*

70 Russia: Captain Guerich, Life Guard Jägerski Regiment, Urshulin, Galicia, 1914
The great coat is the other ranks' pattern with plain collar patches.

Equipment: Standard-pattern officers' equipment with braces, map case, revolver holster, and binoculars.

Weapons: Russian 1909-pattern officers' sword (*Shashka*).

71 Russia: Major General of General Staff Heroys, near Lutsk, Poland, 1916
As General Quartermaster of the Combined Guards Army, Heroys wears the unofficial but very popular *Bekesha* with General's shoulder straps.

Equipment: Standard-pattern officers' waistbelt and sword slings.

Weapons: Russian 1909-pattern officers' sword with gilt metal grip and a miniature St George Cross fitted into the top of the pommel. This type of sword was awarded for bravery and was known as a Golden Weapon.

72 Russia: Junior n.c.o. (Mladshi unter-oficier), Life Guard Ismailovski Regiment, near Lutsk, Poland, 17 November 1916
The issue-pattern winter cap was made of artificial lamb's-wool. The greatcoat collar patches in white indicated the 3rd Regiment in the division. On his breast he wears three St George's Crosses and a St George Medal.

Equipment: Standard infantry equipment with additional bandolier which held thirty rounds (in six clips).

Weapons: Russian 3 line (7·62 mm.) rifle M.1891 with bayonet.

73 Russia: Cossack, 5th Don Cossack Cavalry Regiment, Poland, 1915
The greatcoat for mounted troops was longer and had loose turn-back cuffs with a point at the front and back.

Equipment: Two bandoliers made from black oil cloth: each carried thirty rounds in six clips.

Weapons: Russian 3 line (7·62 mm.) carbine M.1891, and Cossack other ranks' 1881-pattern *shashka*.

74 Russia: Captain (Sotnik) Ojarovski, Terek Cossacks, Lutsk, Poland, 1916
This is typical of the Caucasian dress worn by Cossacks from the Terek and Kuban regions. The badge on the left breast is that of the Elizabethgrad Cavalry School, and the order is St Vladimir 4th Class.

Weapons: Private dagger (*Kindjhal*) and silver mounted sword (*Shashka*).

75 Russia: Colonel (Polkovnik) His Majesty's Life Guard Cossack Regiment, September 1918
This was the only Cossack Regiment, apart from Caucasian, which did not have a stripe or *Lampassen* on its breeches.

Equipment: Standard pattern officers' equipment.

Weapons: Privately purchased, silver-mounted Cossack *Shashka*.

73 Cossack   74 Cossack officer   75 Cossack officer

76 General staff officer   77 Infantry officer   78 Infantryman

76 Russia: Captain of General Staff, Salonika, July 1916

General Staff officers (*Genstabisti*) began to wear a special black tunic. Very little is known about it, and it is considered to have been semi-official, and so existed in many variations.

Equipment: Standard offices' waistbelt.

77 Russia: Colonel (Polkovnik), 3rd Special Purpose Regiment, Salonika, July 1916

Special Purpose Regiments were formed from volunteers for service outside Russia. This regimental commander wears his peace-time cap and breeches. The neck decoration is St Vladimir 3rd Class, and the 4th Class of the same order is worn on the left breast with underneath the badge of the Life Guard Muskovsky Regiment.

Equipment: Officers' waistbelt.

Weapons: Russian 1909-pattern officers' sword.

78 Russia: Private, 4th Special Purpose Regiment, Monastir, November 1916

On arrival in Salonika shortages in clothing and equipment were made good from French stocks, and the new Adrian helmet was issued, as well as a French side cap for wear when the helmet was not required.

Equipment: Since it would be impossible to supply Russian troops with 7·62 mm. ammunition, they received the French rifle and ammunition pouches and braces.

Weapons: French 8 mm. Lebel M.1886/93 rifle and M.1886 (converted) bayonet. The colour of the pennon indicated the number of the regiment in the division, the vertical stripe the company, and the horizontal stripe the battalion, which here is 1st Company, 2nd Battalion, 4th Regiment.

79 Serbia: Private of Infantry, 1916
This typical infantryman wears the issue side cap and greatcoat, and instead of leather ankle boots, traditional peasant *Opanki*.

Equipment: Personal possessions were wrapped in a blanket, and worn as a pack. Over the shoulder is slung a groundsheet, and additional ammunition is carried in a pouch at the back.

Weapons: 7·65 mm. Mauser rifle Model 1893.

80 Serbia: Lieutenant of Artillery, Salonika, 1916
This is the summer light-weight version of the field service uniform which was made from linen or cotton drill. Note the black velvet collar, and black piping around the crown of the kepi which denoted artillery.

Equipment: Binoculars in brown leather case.

81 Serbia: Staff Officer, 1916
The regulation officers' greatcoat was grey with collar patches in arm-of-service colour. This officer does not appear to have worn any badges of rank.

Equipment: Officers' waistbelt and sword slings.

Weapons: Officers' sword.

79 *Infantryman*   80 *Artillery officer*   81 *Staff officer*

82 *Brigadier General*   83 *General*   84 *Staff officer*

82 U.S.A.: Brigadier General (acting) Douglas MacArthur, Commander 84th Brigade, 1918
Homeward bound MacArthur wears a typically fantastic garb. His cap is regulation, but the scarf (knitted by his mother) and fur coat were definitely not.

83 U.S.A.: General John H. Pershing, Commander-in-Chief American Expeditionary Force, Boulogne, June 1917
'Black Jack's' uniform is the standard officers' version of the 1902 olive drab service dress with bronzed buttons and badges.

Equipment: Mounted officers' russet leather garrison belt with pistol magazine pouch.

84 U.S.A.: Colonel Nimon, officer commanding 11th Ammunition Train, France, 1918
The overseas cap with black and gold piping was standard for all officers. Note the rank distinction lace on the greatcoat cuffs. The single inverted gold chevron indicated three months or more service since war was declared east of the 37th meridian west of Greenwich.

85 U.S.A.: Private, 16th Infantry Regiment, France, April 1918
This is the uniform in which the American Expeditionary Force landed in France. The cords on the campaign hat indicated arm of service.

Equipment: M.1910 cartridge belt and water-bottle.

Weapons: U.S. Magazine rifle Cal.30 M.1903.

86 U.S.A.: Corporal Alvin C. York, 82nd Division, Argonne Forest, 8 October 1918
The American hero, winner of the Congressional Medal of Honor, French *Croix de Guerre*, and many other awards, wears the olive drab overseas cap and pattern of greatcoat for non-mounted enlisted men. Based on a photograph taken at Châtel-Chéréry, the scene of his famous raid; York was later promoted to sergeant.

87 U.S.A.: Private of Infantry, winter guard order, 1918
The earflap cap and Mackinaw were made of waterproof cotton duck lined with olive drab cloth. Later patterns had a khaki cloth roll collar.

Equipment: M.1910 cartridge belt.

Weapons: U.S. Magazine rifle Cal.30 M.1903.

85 *Infantryman*   86 *Infantry n.c.o.*   87 *Infantryman*

88 *Pilot officer*   89 *Pilot officer*   90 *Ground crewman*

88 U.S.A.: 2nd Lieutenant Field E. Kindley, 148th Aero Squadron, France, 9 September 1918
Kindley wears regulation officers' service dress with bronzed badges and wings for Military Aviator which was introduced on 15 August 1917.

Equipment: British Sam Browne belt.

89 U.S.A.: Captain 'Eddie' V. Rickenbacker, commander 9th Aero Squadron, Toul, France, September 1918
Rickenbacker wears a British Royal Flying Corps field service cap, Militiary Aviators' wings, and an unofficial squadron badge (butterfly).

Equipment: British Sam Browne belt.

90 U.S.A.: Enlisted man, United States Air Service, France, 1918
At first American troops did not have a summer uniform, and so it was permitted to remove the tunic and wear the khaki flannel shirt, as shirt-sleeve order.